P9-CZV-213

A ROOKIE READER

SANDBOX BETTY

By Catherine Petrie

Illustrations by Sharon Elzaurdia

Prepared under the direction of Robert Hillerich, Ph.D.

 CHILDRENS PRESS, CHICAGO

For Marieke

Library of Congress Cataloging in Publication Data

Petrie, Catherine.
  Sandbox Betty.

  (A Rookie reader)
  Summary: Betty's sandcastles are the tallest,
  neatest, and best of all. Includes word list.
  [1. Sandcastles — Fiction.   2. Stories in rhyme]
  I. Elzaurdia, Sharon, ill.   II. Title.   III. Series.
  PZ8.3.P457 San   [E]   81-15547
  ISBN 0-516-03578-9   AACR2

Copyright © 1982 by Regensteiner Publishing Enterprises, Inc.
All rights reserved. Published simultaneously in Canada.
Printed in the United States of America.
     4 5 6 7 8 9 10 R 91 90 89 88 87 86 85 84

Sandbox Betty

builds them TALL.

Wall to wall, she builds them TALL.

She builds them well.

9

She builds them swell.

Of all the rest, hers is BEST.

Sandbox Betty knows it all!

They are neat.
Can't be beat.

Neat and tall, they never fall.

She builds them well.

She builds them swell.

24

Of all the rest ...

hers is BEST.

Sandbox Betty knows it all!

WORD LIST

all	from	rest
and	hers	sand
are	how	Sandbox Betty
be	is	she
beat	it	swell
best	knows	tall
builds	learn	the
can't	make	them
castles	neat	they
fall	never	to
free	of	wall
	or	well

About the Author

Catherine Petrie is a reading specialist with a Master of Science degree in Reading. She has been teaching reading in the public school system for the past ten years. Her experience as a teacher has made her aware of the lack of material currently available for the very young reader. Her creative use of a limited vocabulary based on high-frequency sight words, combined with frequent repetition and rhyming word families, provide the beginning reader with a positive independent reading experience. *Hot Rod Harry, Sandbox Betty,* and *Joshua James Likes Trucks* are her first published beginning readers.

About the Artist

Sharon Elzaurdia received a Bachelor of Fine Arts degree from the University of Illinois. After graduation, she worked for eight years as a designer and illustrator in a graphic arts studio. She has illustrated many children's textbooks and trade books.

Mrs. Elzaurdia lives with her husband Bill and three children in a suburb of Chicago, where she has taught gymnastics, swimming, and crafts to young children.